ACTORS ON SHAKESPEARE

Macbeth HARRIET WALTER

Harriet Walter trained at LAMDA and began her career with touring political groups such as 7:84 and Joint Stock. She joined the Royal Shakespeare Company in 1981 and is now an associate artist. Between stage work and radio recordings she has so far played some 15 Shakespearean roles including Juliet, Ophelia, two Helenas, Portia, Viola, Imogen, Gonerill, Beatrice and Lady Macbeth. Besides Shakespeare, her stage work has ranged from Webster to Chekhov and Ibsen, to contemporary work by Pinter, Stoppard, Yasmina Reza, Howard Barker, Simon Gray, Timberlake Wertenbaker, Caryl Churchill, David Hare, David Edgar and Stephen Poliakoff.

Harriet has also appeared in several feature films including *The Governess*, Louis Malle's *Milou en Mai* and *Sense and Sensibility*; and on television she starred in *The Price*, *The Dorothy L. Sayers Mysteries* (as Harriet Vane), *The Men's Room*, *Unfinished Business* and Ian McEwan's *The Imitation Game*.

Harriet's book on acting, *Other People's Shoes*, is published by Penguin and she has contributed several essays and articles to other drama publications.

Colin Nicholson is the originator and editor for the Actors on Shakespeare series published by Faber and Faber.

HARRIET WALTER

Macbeth

Series Editor: Colin Nicholson

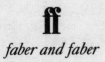

faber and faber

First published in 2002
by Faber and Faber Limited
3 Queen Square London WC1N 3AU

Typeset by Faber and Faber in Minion
Printed in England by Mackays of Chatham plc

A CIP record for this book is available from the British Library

ISBN 0–571–21407–X

10 9 8 7 6 5 4 3 2 1

Introduction

Shakespeare: Playwright, Actor and Actors' Playwright

It is important to remember that William Shakespeare was an actor, and his understanding of the demands and rewards of acting helped him as a playwright to create roles of such richness and depth that actors in succeeding generations – even those with no reason or desire to call themselves 'classical' actors – have sought opportunities to perform them.

As the company dramatist, Shakespeare was writing under the pressure of producing scripts for almost immediate performance by his fellow players – the Lord Chamberlain's Men (later the King's Men), who, as a share-holding group, had a vested interest in their playhouse. Shakespeare was writing for a familiar set of actors: creating roles for particular players to interpret; and, being involved in a commercial enterprise, he was sensitive to the direct contact between player and audience and its power to bring in paying customers. His answer to the challenge produced a theatrical transformation: Shakespeare peopled the stage with highly credible personalities, men and women who were capable of change, and recognizable as participants in the human condition which their audience also shared. He connected two new and important elements: the idea of genuine individuality – the solitary, reflecting, self-communing soul, which is acutely aware of its own sufferings and desires; and, correlatively, the idea of inner life as something that not only exists but can also be explored. For him, the connection became the motor of dramatic action on the stage, as it is the motor of personal action in real life.

The primary importance of the actor cannot be disputed: it is his or her obligation – assisted to a greater or lesser extent by a director's overall vision of the play – to understand the personality they are representing onstage, and the nature of the frictions taking place when that personality interacts with other characters in the drama. Shakespeare's achievement goes far beyond the creation of memorable characters (Macbeth, Falstaff) to embrace the exposition of great relationships (Macbeth–Lady Macbeth; Falstaff–Prince Hal). Great roles require great actors, and there is no group of people in a better position to interpret those roles to *us* than the principal actors of *our* generation – inhabitants of a bloodline whose vigour resonates from the sixteenth century to the present day – who have immersed themselves in the details of Shakespeare's creations and have been party to their development through rehearsal and performance.

Watching Shakespeare can be an intimidating experience, especially for those who are not well versed in the text, or in the conventions of the Elizabethan stage. Many excellent books have been written for the academic market but our aim in this series is somewhat different. *Actors on Shakespeare* asks contemporary performers to choose a play of particular interest to them, push back any formal boundaries that may obstruct channels of free communication and give the modern audience a fresh, personal view. Naturally the focus for each performer is different – and these diverse volumes are anything but uniform in their approach to the task – but their common intention is, primarily, to look again at plays that some audiences may know well and others not at all, as well as providing an insight into the making of a performance.

Each volume works in its own right, without assuming an in-depth knowledge of the play, and uses substantial quotation to contextualize the principal points. The fresh approach of the many and varied writers will, we hope, enhance your enjoyment of Shakespeare's work.

Colin Nicholson
February 2002

Note: For reference, the text used here is the Arden Shakespeare.

Characters

Duncan, *King of Scotland*
Malcolm *and* Donalbain, *his sons*
Macbeth
Lady Macbeth
Banquo, Macduff, Lenox, Ross, Menteth, Angus, Cathness,
    noblemen of Scotland
Lady Macduff
Her Son
Siward, *Earl of Northumberland*
Young Siward, *his son*
Fleance, *Banquo's son*
Seyton
Witches
Captain, Doctors, Gentlewoman, Hecate, Murderers,
    Old Man, Porter, Sergeant

Macbeth was performed by the Royal Shakespeare Company at Stratford-upon-Avon in November 1999, with the following cast:

Macbeth	Antony Sher
Lady Macbeth	Harriet Walter
Weird Sisters	Noma Dumezweni
	Polly Kemp
	Diane Beck
Duncan	Joseph O'Connor
Malcolm	John Dougall
Banquo	Ken Bones
Macduff	Nigel Cooke
Lady Macduff	Diane Beck
Ross	Paul Webster
Porter	Stephen Noonan
Doctor	Trevor Martin
Gentlewoman	Polly Kemp

Directed by Greg Doran

My Dearest Partner of Greatness

Foreword

The tragedy of *Macbeth* is set in motion by two people, a man and his wife. None of it would have happened if either had been acting alone. To understand the play it is necessary to anatomize the partnership that motors it.

In 1999 I was cast as Lady Macbeth in Greg Doran's production of the play with Antony Sher in the lead. Like Hamlet or Falstaff, Lady Macbeth is so much part of our cultural landscape that she seems actually to exist somewhere out there. Throughout the world her name is a byword for monstrosity – the unnatural woman, the evil power behind the throne. Even after I have played her, the archetype remains – a towering Siddons-like shadow, impervious to my interpretation. However, in September 1999 I had a practical need to find the human being behind the icon, and I had to find her within myself.

In the months leading up to rehearsals I read and re-read the play with as open a mind as possible and pored over other actresses' accounts of playing the part. It was both comforting and exhilarating to commune with these ghosts, to feel part of a tiny band of people who had shared this rare and particular task down the years; but in the end I felt nearer to them than to Lady Macbeth. She remained like a mountainous wave that would break over me and crush me unless I caught it and rode it. The only way to find my own Lady Macbeth (apart from through the mysterious workings of an actor's subconscious) was to get up in rehearsals, say her words and start interacting with Antony Sher.

Rehearsals

The first thing that Greg Doran did on day one of rehearsals was to blast away any superstition surrounding the play. The performance history of the play is reputedly littered with misfortune, ranging from slapstick accidents to a supposed intervention of evil forces, all of which support the superstition that the play is jinxed and that the 'M'-word must not be uttered in a theatre building. Theories abound as to the origins of the superstition, but Greg favoured the most practical one in circulation, namely that because so much of the play takes place at night in semi-darkness, an above average number of falls and breakages can occur. In fact, according to Greg, the play's history is no more steeped in catastrophe than any other's – maybe even less so – and to illustrate his point (and put the newly assembled group of almost-strangers at ease) he cited some famous stage disasters involving quite other Shakespeare plays. Curses are an act of faith, as so much else was at this stage of the game; so if we all together scoffed at the *Macbeth* Curse, it would no longer exist. Hecate, like Tinkerbell, would die if no one believed in her. '*Macbeth, Macbeth,*' we boldly repeated wherever we went. To hell with 'The Scottish Play'!

On a more serious level, we discussed our varying attitudes to the supernatural. It is such a strong strand in the play that we could not skim over it, however comfortable it would have been to do so. The three weird sisters are a fact of the play; so are the apparitions that haunt Macbeth. The important thing was not so much what we individually believed as what we could make a contemporary 'Western materialist' audience believe.

3

For all our scientific rationality, modern society still acknowledges that there are forces we cannot explain. Some people believe in supernatural phenomena – in ghosts and witches and evil forces – others would explain everything as being generated from within the human mind. With Greg's leadership and our consent, this production of *Macbeth* took the rationalist psychological line. In one way this was the easier line to get a modern audience to swallow, though by 'easier' I do not mean more comfortable. Few propositions can be less comfortable than that the evil in *Macbeth* stems from human nature and from no other source. Anyway, what was the alternative? To compete with Hollywood special effects and create some extraterrestrial spooks, now the stuff of family entertainment?

Most people acknowledge the existence of human powers that are 'super'-natural or 'extra'-sensory. There have always been people who can see the future or sense what someone else is feeling; and, after much discussion, in the first weeks of rehearsal, our witches started to evolve from this kind of territory.

In certain cultures where witchcraft remains integral to society there is no dichotomy between the supernatural and the natural. In the Zulu version of the play, *Umabatha*, for instance, the witches credibly straddle both worlds. However, in the West we have all but completely severed the connection between the practical and the spiritual sides of our nature. We either rationalize witchcraft or mock it. In Britain we have the added problem of an audience having seen *Macbeth* countless times, often in very unconvincing renditions. 'Hubble bubble, toil and trouble,' has become a comic-book joke. Our production would have to tap into some force, some communal fear, that would have the equivalent effect on our audience to that of witches on a Jacobean one.

Shakespeare himself had to make adjustments to keep up with stage fashion. Originally he had three devils in place of the weird sisters, but the theatrical currency of devils was already starting to devalue through overuse, and they were more likely to induce laughter than fear. James I, who was on the throne when *Macbeth* was written, famously believed in witches; yet even during the lifetime of the play attitudes to stage witches shifted and they started down the same comic route as the devils before them. Perhaps that is why no one in the spoken text of *Macbeth* uses the word 'witch'. (There is one exception, in Act I, scene iii, when the First Witch cites an insult against herself: '"Aroynt thee, witch!" the rump-fed ronyon cries' – and the sailor's wife who delivered it will pay for the underestimation.) As Charles Lamb said of Shakespeare's Weird Sisters, '[they] are serious things. Their presence cannot coincide with mirth.'

So what forces do we fear? One of the most primitive fears we all share is fear of darkness. Most of the scenes in *Macbeth* take place at night and it is darkness that gives the night its potency. As Macbeth puts it when the clock strikes two in the morning,

> Now o'er the one half-world
> Nature seems dead, and wicked dreams abuse
> The curtain'd sleep.
>
> (Act II, scene i)

Intrinsically connected to night's predominance over the play is the state of sleeplessness, and the unnatural apparitions that so disturb Macbeth come to him in those strange, unreal hours between night and morning when, as Lady Macbeth says, the night is 'Almost at odds with morning, which is which'. But darkness in *Macbeth* is not necessarily a literal darkness caused by night; it is a metaphorical darkness, a state of distorted visions and disturbed minds, projected on to the physical world. In one of the only scenes featuring a relatively detached commentator on the events of the play, Act II, scene iv, an Old Man, remarks that, among other troubling signs,

> by th' clock 'tis day,
> And yet dark night strangles the travelling lamp.
> Is 't night's predominance, or the day's shame,
> That darkness does the face of earth entomb,
> When living light should kiss it?

According to Greg, the word 'fear' appears more often in *Macbeth* than in any other Shakespeare play, and the word 'love' least often. (In trying to check this out, I discovered that nearly all references to love are made by the King or in his presence, and I also noticed that it is often used hypocritically.) It is a dark and loveless play, and we would make it literally so. A priority would be to try to achieve total blackout for certain moments – notably at the very beginning of the play – which would involve putting out the green neon exit signs for a second or so. We foresaw some battles with theatre-licensing authorities, but felt it was worth it.

The scenery would be minimal. The walls and stairs would be black, as would most of the costumes. Rare demonstrations of love and natural light would be all the more emphatic as contrasts. (Blinding images from the final production included the white-robed King at his last prayers and Lady Macduff bathing her children surrounded by freshly blanched laundry.) Greg pointed out that Shakespeare gives clear guidelines for a lighting designer all along the way. In Act IV, scene iii, often known as the 'England Scene', the exiled Malcolm invites Macduff: 'Let us seek out some desolate shade, and there / Weep our sad bosoms empty,' which suggests the pervading glare of an English summer's day. It is the first respite from the godless claustrophobia of Scotland, and it comes well over halfway through the play.

The important thing about darkness is what it allows our imaginations to see. Many productions of *Macbeth* have fallen down because nothing the set-designer might come up with could match the fearsome pictures conjured up by Shakespeare's words. (For this reason, *Macbeth* works exceptionally well on the radio.)

So on that first day of rehearsal we had touched on the supernatural, fear of darkness – and what else? Oh yes . . . blood. According to Jan Kott, 'A production of *Macbeth* not evoking a picture of the world flooded with blood would inevitably be false.'* Despite the fact that he was writing in the sixties, before audiences had become (literally, sometimes) saturated with risible amounts of stage gore, the comment worried me. Greg had proposed that we keep demonstrations of blood to a minimum. I read and re-read the wise man Kott's statement, hoping for a reconciliation of the two men's ideas. Then I saw it: the word 'evoking'. That let us off the hook. In studio theatre's terms, in front of virtually schlock-proof school audiences, Greg's 'less' might very well *evoke* more. What was emerging from discussion was that the terror of the play is of a psychological rather than a physical nature. The mind of the murderer is more frightening than the murder itself.

As homework for the end of our first week, Greg set us two tasks. First, we were to bring in any images, photos or whatever that contained something of how we saw our characters. It did not need to be a literal idea for a costume; it could be a famous person who had some essence in common with the

* *Shakespeare Our Contemporary*, University Paperbacks, Methuen (1996).

7

part. Secondly, we were each to think what truly terrified us and bring some illustrative story to the rest of the cast. As was hoped, this exercise tapped something personal and authentic, which helped us all avoid generalized 'frightened acting' when it came to performance.

The rest of the week was given over to verse-speaking workshops, physical preparations for fights, introductory drumming and singing sessions (since these skills were to be integral to the production) for half of the day, and a slow reading aloud of the play during the second half.

Looking for Clues

For the read-through we took roles in order round the table, changing the cast for each scene, with the sole proviso that we were never to read our own part. This enabled us to study the play objectively and to highlight things about our character by listening to another voice reading it.

Shakespeare packs the beginning of the play chock-full of character clues hidden in the language and our ears began to tune in to them. Just to give one example: in the first scene the witches chant, 'Fair is foul, and foul is fair,' and two scenes later Macbeth's first line is: 'So foul and fair a day I have not seen.' This is obviously a deliberate echo, since Shakespeare was never short of adjectives. So what effect did he want it to have? To show Macbeth's susceptibility? Or the witches' insight into Macbeth's state of mind? The effect need not be nailed down at this stage, just recognized.

I wanted to notch up all the data I could about my husband. Lady Macbeth thinks she knows him pretty well, and to discover whether she was right I needed to know him at least as well. I had the advantage now of learning about him on the battlefield – the only arena in which Lady Macbeth does not observe him first-hand. In Act I, scene ii I heard much of 'brave Macbeth (well he deserves that name)' and of 'noble Macbeth'. I heard him compared with eagles and lions and heard the King exclaim of him, 'O valiant cousin! worthy gentleman!' I heard my husband described as 'Bellona's bridegroom', which – in jest – supplied the company with my missing first name, but more seriously told me that Macbeth is a soldier wedded to the Goddess of War.

I heard how my husband,

Disdaining Fortune, with his brandish'd steel,
Which smok'd with bloody execution,
Like Valour's minion, carved out his passage
Till he fac'd the slave;

then

> unseamed him from the nave to th' chops,
And fix'd his head upon our battlements.

I also heard how, in the thick of the enemy, my husband was

Nothing afeard of what [himself] didst make,
Strange images of death.

  (Act I, scene iii)

In other words, Macbeth was butchering the enemy left, right and centre and was untouched by the horrid sights he was creating. All of this to be compared with his later terror at the image of the murdered King.

At the start of the play events follow one another at such terrifying speed that both audience and characters can barely catch their breath. I emphasize this breakneck speed because it is almost a clue in itself. (For one thing, it explains the Macbeths' flawed and haphazard plan for the King's murder: they barely have time to discuss it.)

In the few scenes leading to Macbeth's return home, we hear the witches announce their plan to meet with him. Then we get a first-hand report from the battlefield, the news of Cawdor's treachery and the King's pledge to give his titles to 'noble Macbeth'. Back to the witches (Act I, scene iii), lurking in wait on the blasted heath, and the first triumphant entrance of the much-talked-about captains Macbeth and Banquo. The witches greet Macbeth as Thane of Glamis (his ancestral title), which he knows himself to be, then Thane of Cawdor, which we know from scene ii he is about to become but about which Macbeth knows nothing yet; and the third greeting – 'All hail, Macbeth! that shalt be King hereafter.' – surprises everyone.

The Thane of Ross enters and confirms the first prophecy. Somewhere round here Macbeth writes to his wife, telling her all the news so far, then goes to meet the King. The ex-Thane of Cawdor has been put to death. King Duncan names his son Malcolm heir to the throne and invites himself to stay that night with Macbeth and his wife.

It is noticeable how in their first encounter with the witches it is Banquo who takes the initiative. He steps into the hollow created by Macbeth's silence. Unlike Macbeth, Banquo treats the witches as a bit of a joke. Their business is with Macbeth, but since he 'seems rapt withal', Banquo asks them: 'Speak then to me, who neither beg, nor fear, / Your favours nor your hate'; and when he learns that his children will be kings, he does not seem about to act on the news. Macbeth, by contrast, is profoundly shaken.

Why indeed does Macbeth 'start, and seem to fear / Things that do sound so fair', as Banquo puts it when the witches have spoken? The answer is that their prophecy comes uncannily close to what he has secretly willed, and that offers terrifying prospects. In Banquo, Shakespeare offers us a character to offset against Macbeth, rather as Horatio throws light on Hamlet by being the more 'normal' person. Banquo and Macbeth are equal-ranking captains both prized by the King. As his consort on the battlefield, Banquo knows Macbeth almost as intimately as Lady Macbeth does. He is quick to observe all of Macbeth's reactions but cannot yet guess at his thoughts. He does warn Macbeth that

> oftentimes, to win us to our harm,
> The instruments of Darkness tell us truths;
> Win us with honest trifles, to betray's
> In deepest consequence –

but – and here the actor has a choice of how emphatically to play the lines – he seems happy to let it go at that, turning immediately to take Ross and Angus aside with: 'Cousins, a word, I pray you.'

Macbeth says very little in his first few scenes. Like Hamlet, he first speaks at any length in soliloquy to the audience. In the witches' presence he seems to be in a trance, and not until they have already vanished into the air does he regain his tongue to call them back and tell him more:

> By Sinel's death, I know, I am Thane of Glamis;
> But how of Cawdor? the Thane of Cawdor lives . . .

He seems to question not so much the prophecy itself as the means by which it is to come about.

I found it significant that the first aspect of the prophecy to be picked up by Macbeth once he and Banquo were alone was: 'Your children shall be kings.' This was a note to store up for the future.

There are clues also in what is not said. Given his first chance to speak to the audience, Macbeth does not say, 'This is dangerous nonsense,' but (my emphasis):

> Two *truths* are told,
> As happy prologues to the swelling act
> Of the imperial theme.

We will discover Macbeth to be a reasoning man, but in this case his desire to believe overcomes his reason.

I suspect that if you were to ask the person-in-the-street

what they knew of Lady Macbeth, most who knew anything would say something like: 'She's the one who persuades her husband to kill the King . . .' But I was finding indications in the text that Lady Macbeth does not put the idea of killing the King into her husband's head; it is already there. There is a huge difference between coercing a totally upright person to commit a crime and working on the wavering will of someone who already wants to commit that crime but fears the consequences. I was not out to clear Lady Macbeth's name, but I wanted to straighten out a few facts.

In performance, vital words can be missed, especially if they come early in the play when the audience's ears may not yet be tuned in to Shakespeare's language. In Macbeth's first soliloquy they may not completely grasp:

My thought, whose murder yet is but fantastical,
Shakes so my single state of man,
That function is smother'd in surmise,
And nothing is, but what is not.

(Act I, scene iii)

or Macbeth's reaction a little later when the king proclaims Malcolm heir to the throne and Prince of Cumberland:

The Prince of Cumberland! – That is a step
On which I must fall down, or else o'erleap,
For in my way it lies.

(Act I, scene iv)

By 'eavesdropping' on Macbeth's soliloquies I realized how well his wife had got him taped. In her first scene she addresses her absent husband:

Thou'dst have, great Glamis,
That which cries, 'Thus thou must do,' if thou have it;

And that which rather thou dost fear to do,
Than wishest should be undone.

   (Act I, scene v)

Compare that with his later

     If th' assassination
Could trammel up the consequence, and catch
With his surcease success; that but this blow
Might be the be-all and the end-all . . .

   (Act I, scene vii)

He would be happy to rely on Fate: 'If Chance will have me King, why, Chance may crown me, / Without my stir' (Act I, scene iii).

And he *can* count on advancement without any stir. Shortly after this speech, the King assures him: 'I have begun to plant thee, and will labour / To make thee full of growing,' and repeats this sentiment to Lady Macbeth in Act I, scene vi: 'we love him highly, / And shall continue our graces towards him.' So what's the problem? The problem is that ordinary old advancement isn't enough. The witches have planted in Macbeth the idea of becoming king, and now nothing less than that will do.

Shakespeare repeatedly uses the image of planting and it is an apt one. Macbeth and Lady Macbeth are caught at a moment of ripeness and preparedness for evil. The witches are agents of this evil and for that reason they do not seek out Banquo, who proves less fertile soil, but Macbeth. Lady Macbeth understands her husband as well as the witches do and builds on the work they have begun. She herself never kills; but if she had let well alone, Macbeth would not have acted. That is the considerable extent of her blame.

I had already scoured the text for any insights into Lady Macbeth as an individual, separate from her husband; but except for the odd 'honour'd hostess' or 'fair and noble hostess' from the King, no one comments on her or throws any light on her character. Nobody seems to know her. She has no confidante. Her world is confined to the castle and its servants, but it was hard for my imagination to people the place or fill it with domestic goings-on. A Lady Macbeth busying herself with the housekeeping, or taking tea with a circle of friends, just did not ring true. It didn't ring true, because Shakespeare's creation seems to exist only within the time-frame of the play. It was as though she had visited Shakespeare's imagination fully formed, giving away no secrets – and therein lies a lot of her power. Back to the clues in the text.

Wound up and ready for action, Lady Macbeth bursts on to the stage reading her husband's letter.

'They met me in the day of success; and I have learn'd by the perfect'st report, they have more in them than mortal knowledge. When I burn'd in desire to question them further, they made themselves air, into which they vanish'd. Whiles I stood rapt in the wonder of it, came missives from the King, who all-hail'd me "Thane of Cawdor"; by which title, before, these Weïrd Sisters saluted me, and referr'd me to the coming on of time, with "Hail, king that shalt be!" This have I thought good to deliver thee (my dearest partner of greatness) that thou might'st not lose the dues of rejoicing, by being ignorant of what greatness is promis'd thee. Lay it to thy heart, and farewell.'

(Act I, scene v)

Having read her husband's letter, she too leaps to believe the prophecy: 'Glamis thou art, and Cawdor; and shalt be / What thou art promis'd.' However, she believes that 'fate and metaphysical aid' only '*seem* [my emphasis] / To have [him] crown'd withal,' and that the couple must give Fate a helping hand.

My Dearest Partner of Greatness

In listening to Macbeth's soliloquies I also discovered how closely Lady Macbeth and her lord mirror one another's thoughts and language. (I would return to this again and again as the play went on, using Macbeth's speeches to help me fathom his increasingly silent partner's state of mind.) By means of these echoes of imagery shared between husband and wife Shakespeare subliminally suggests a twinning of minds. Note the cross-over of imagery between Macbeth's

> Stars, hide your fires!
> Let not light see my black and deep desires;
> The eye wink at the hand; yet let that be,
> Which the eye fears, when it is done, to see.
>
> (Act I, scene iv)

and Lady Macbeth's

> Come, thick Night,
> And pall thee in the dunnest smoke of Hell,
> That my keen knife see not the wound it makes,
> Nor Heaven peep through the blanket of the dark,
> To cry 'Hold, hold!'
>
> (Act I, scene v)

If the eye is sentinel to the conscience and the hand is the instrument of action, then to commit evil the two must be kept apart. The disembodied hand acts on its own beyond the responsibility of its 'owner': 'I don't know what came over me, Inspector; my finger just suddenly pulled the trigger.' The schism between thought and deed is a familiar Shakespearean theme. As Hamlet says, 'the native hue of resolution / Is sicklied o'er with the pale cast of thought.'

Macbeth and Hamlet would have agreed on much at the beginning of the play, but while Macbeth has become a murderer by Act II, scene ii, Hamlet remains the philosopher to the end. Hamlet's toughest resolution is still expressed in terms of thoughts rather than deeds: 'from this time forth, / My thoughts be bloody or be nothing worth' (*Hamlet*, Act IV, scene iv).

By contrast, when Macbeth, also in Act IV, says,

> From this moment,
> The very firstlings of my heart shall be
> The firstlings of my hand.
>
> (Act IV, scene i)

we know he will act on his words.

How differently would things have turned out if Hamlet had been married to Lady Macbeth? This is not a frivolous question. *Macbeth* is, among other things, the portrait of a *folie à deux*. It deals with the unique and deadly chemistry between two particular individuals. If Lady Macbeth were pure demoness, she could make a murderer of anyone, even Hamlet; but she isn't. The materials have to be right, and Macbeth's personality fits. She knows him like her own skin. (Incidentally, Hamlet, being a woman-blamer, would probably have bleated that it was all his wife's fault – something Macbeth never does.)

When husband and wife first meet on stage, they have no need to spell things out. Macbeth has three lines in the scene. He has paved much of the way in his letter. Although if anyone had intercepted it they would have found nothing incriminating, to Lady Macbeth's fertile ear it reads: 'The way is clear, my dearest partner of greatness, and I know you will know what to do.' All he has to say when he greets her is: 'My dearest love, / Duncan comes here tonight.'

We have already been party to Lady Macbeth's extreme reaction to the same news earlier, and now she can afford a calm 'And when goes hence?' (There is something of a test going on here, as though she is really asking: 'And is he going to leave here alive, do you think? If not, what are you going to do about it?')

He replies, 'Tomorrow, as he purposes.'

So far, so innocent, if the room were bugged. But why add 'as he purposes'? A simple 'Tomorrow' would have done. In the husband-and-wife telepathy this added phrase means: 'At least that is what *he* thinks,' and that is enough of a cue for Lady Macbeth to pounce in with: 'O! never / Shall sun that morrow see!'

Then Shakespeare builds two beats of silence into the five-beat line, during which . . . what? It is a truly pregnant pause. Husband and wife search one another's faces, hold their breath in shock. The thoughts they had dared think alone are now brought literally face to face. It is *the* moment. The time is right, and what has hitherto been safe fantasy is in danger of happening. Both are terrified, but she is better at covering it up. Her next words dictate something of how the actor must play Macbeth in that moment: 'Your face, my Thane, is as a book, where men / May read strange matters.'

This has a doubly ironic ring, if the audience remembers King Duncan's observation in the previous scene that 'There's no art / To find the mind's construction in the face,' seconds before a seemingly loyal Macbeth enters and kneels at his feet. Now, Lady Macbeth warns her husband that he is see-through and must learn to 'look like th' innocent flower, / But be the serpent under't.'

She must tread carefully with her husband, whom she thinks is 'too full o' th' milk of human kindness, / To catch the nearest way'. In soliloquy, before his arrival, she could apostrophize him and say,

> Thou wouldst be great;
> Art not without ambition, but without
> The illness should attend it: what thou wouldst highly,
> That wouldst thou holily; wouldst not play false,
> And yet wouldst wrongly win;
>> (Act I, scene iv)

but she knows better than to tell these truths to his face. Instead she merely says:

> He that's coming
> Must be provided for; and you shall put
> This night's great business into my dispatch.
>> (Act I, scene v)

By taking the responsibility on herself she trips him into action, hoping to bypass his conscience.

Apart from in his letter to her, the Macbeths never mention the word 'King' when talking of Duncan. (Lady Macbeth uses it only once later in the play when referring to her husband, and he likewise later, and only in the witches' presence.) Nor do they venture the word 'murder', but skirt round it with euphemisms. She talks of 'This night's great business' and 'our great quell'. Neither can confront the symbolic enormity of killing a king.

Lady Macbeth has been described as more pragmatic, more ruthless and more courageous than Macbeth, but she has summoned these qualities out of necessity, to serve her 'fell purpose'. Courage breeds courage. She dares Heaven itself to prevent her plan, and when no obvious divine intervention is forthcoming, she feels omnipotent. However, unlike Macbeth, she does not dare look deep into herself, where she would find a much more fearful creature.

She has also been called unimaginative. That would account for her boldness, but it also diminishes it. To be unimaginative is to know no fear, and those with no fear cannot be called courageous. I prefer to think that she deliberately narrows her focus, shutting out all speculation about the future in order to act more efficiently. When she begs the spirits: 'unsex me here'and, 'make thick my blood, / Stop up th' access and passage to remorse,' she is praying for her natural imaginative susceptibility to be suppressed. For me, the journey of the part of Lady Macbeth is the fracturing and final disintegration of that suppression. In Act I, scene v she needs to see herself as the braver of the pair, whose role is to

> pour my spirits in thine ear,
> And chastise with the valour of my tongue
> All that impedes thee from the golden round ...

Indeed, most of Lady Macbeth's valour lies in her tongue. Words embolden her until they become deeds. As events progress, she has less and less to say. Her courage slips as her words dry up.

She does lack imagination in those areas where she lacks the experience of her husband. She has not seen blood shed in battle, nor developed Macbeth's sense of soldierly honour; nor has she his reputation to lose. As a consequence, she thinks she is better equipped for killing than she proves to be. This is neatly illustrated by the contrast between her superficial boldness immediately after the murder of Duncan – 'My hands are of your colour; but I shame / To wear a heart so white' (Act II, scene ii) – and the betrayal of her true reaction in the sleepwalking scene much later: 'Yet who would have thought the old man had so much blood in him?' (Act V, scene i).

When Lady Macbeth welcomes Duncan to the castle, she performs the 'innocent flower' to perfection. This is eased by ritual and courtly language, which need give nothing away. She has to brave out receiving the King's gentle compliments, but once that ordeal is passed she can congratulate herself on her smooth success at the first hurdle.

This success and her exhilaration at it fuel her fury at Macbeth's behaviour in the next scene. He signally fails at the first hurdle, rushes away from the banquet that he is supposed to host, and when his wife catches up with him, tells her they can't go through with it. She has made her decision and is geared up for the kill – and I discovered further reasons why she could not possibly drop out now.

A Macbeth for Our Times

The point is not to modernize a classic play for the sake of it, or to be trendy, but each generation coins its own definitions of war, nationhood, morality etc., and while it is important to take into account the times that formed the play, a production must be as much about the era in which it is played, if it is to be living theatre rather than an acted-out story from days of yore.

'Modernizing' Shakespeare can be achieved without updating costumes or props, by means of a company intelligence connecting with the themes of the play and breathing present-day meaning into an ancient text. This we hoped to do with *Macbeth*, but after two weeks of research and discussions it was felt that our production would benefit from some modern visual aids to help nail some of the extraordinarily contemporary analogies we had found, and to shake up some of the preconceptions that clung to such a famous play.

However, we wanted to avoid too specific a modern context. Television has produced a rather literal-minded audience and what we did not want was comments like: 'Oh I see: Macbeth is Slobodan Milosevic and Lady M is his missus'; or, 'Why doesn't Macbeth e-mail his wife?' or, 'Why are they all carrying candles?' We ended up with a recognizably modern but still metaphorical world where power-lines were down and nightmare hallucinations hovered in the candlelight.

It also needed to be a world where (as in the historical Scotland) the king's successor was appointed from his chiefs and not yet by the automatic rule of primogeniture. If Scotland had been a stable hierarchy, Macbeth might have been satisfied with any place near the top of it; but in the world we were trying to create, a world of bloody scraps between tribal factions (to which, since the break-up of Yugoslavia and the USSR, a modern audience would easily relate), Macbeth could argue that if he did not make a grab for power now, he might be knocked out of the running for ever.

A generation or two ago, in the aftermath of World War II, Britons could relate to the notion of a war that could be ended with a lasting peace, secured by a Good King. Fifty years and hundreds of wars later, not even the relatively blessed British can feel so confident. The peace that Malcolm brings at the end of *Macbeth* feels temporary, and in our production this was underlined by a reminder of unfinished business – the boy Fleance appeared right at the end, just as the figure of Banquo rose from the kneeling crowd round Malcolm and looked into his son's eyes.

Whether or not Shakespeare himself fought a war, his psychology is, as usual, impeccable. In our research we watched documentary film footage of revenge killings and massacres, talked to some Kosovan refugees; Tony Sher and I talked to a psychiatrist about psychopaths and post-traumatic stress disorder and Tony interviewed a couple of murderers. Everything we learned from these is borne out in the play.

One documentary showed American GIs training for duty in Vietnam. Aside from the physical toughness of the programme, days and months of being bellowed at beat the questioning man out of them and whipped them into rage-filled killing machines. The massacre of a whole village of women, children and old men in My Lai was possible only because of such training.

One soldier, when interviewed about My Lai, talked of 'psyching' himself up then 'blanking out' as he mowed his victims down. A similar process was described by one of the murderers whom Tony met, and this proved useful for the 'Is this a dagger . . .?' speech in Act II, scene i.

Incidents like My Lai cross the moral line between killing that is acceptable – even praised – in war, and plain murder. The GIs who 'survived' My Lai had been turned into murderers and rapists. They may have 'blanked out' while killing, but the sights and deeds they had suppressed would revisit them in flashbacks and nightmares for the rest of their lives. According to the psychiatrist whom we consulted, one of the clues that identify a psychopath is an unflinching reaction when confronted with their victim. Had the Macbeths been straightforward 'evil' psychopaths, they would have experienced no remorse for their crimes and no post-traumatic symptoms. The fact that Macbeth experiences hallucinations and flashbacks, and that Lady Macbeth sleepwalks are signs that they are normally functioning human beings.

Shakespeare makes the connection between seeing the victim and consequent remorse in several ways. The agents of evil to whom Lady Macbeth appeals dwell in 'sightless substances' (and I have already referred to the pivotal moment when Lady Macbeth sets eyes on the murdered King). When Macbeth makes his direst resolution to kill Macduff's wife and children he says,

> No boasting like a fool;
> This deed I'll do, before this purpose cool:
> But no more sights!
> (Act IV, scene i)

He knows that accomplishment of the deed requires a moral blindfold. Ever since seeing the slaughtered King, Macbeth has needed someone else to do his killing for him – just as today's military leaders conduct their wars by increasingly remote control.

In the 1990s, images of the Balkan wars were extra shocking because primitive holocaust was set against a sophisticated European backdrop. Something of this juxtaposition was echoed in our production.

The decision to present the play in modern dress was a relatively late one and it alarmed me at first. I recognized all the benefits elsewhere, but in the case of Lady Macbeth I had some adjusting to do. Firstly the question of image. The men for the most part would be in neutralizing uniform or evening dress. Female costume is more tied up with fashion and that starts to pin one down to a specific date, class and type. When Greg asked us to bring in magazine and newspaper cuttings that had some flavour of our character, I brought in a collection that ranged from a sleek model through Bernadette Devlin to a photo of a haunted Lenin nearing his deathbed. All of these had some element of Lady Macbeth. No one of them summed her up. I wanted to inhabit that same non-specific land as the flak-jacketed or dinner-jacketed men. I did not want to have to choose whether she was more Armani than Donna Karan. My problem was eliminated by the designer Stephen Brimson Lewis whizzing up a non-intrusive classical look just for my Lady Macbeth.

There were further anomalies for Lady Macbeth in a modern-dress production. A lot of the rationale I was building to explain her behaviour was rooted in her remoteness from power. In a modern world she could have ruled a country or a corporation and had no need to operate through her husband. The other theme that was to become central to Tony's and my interpretations was that of childlessness, and for my interior psychological map this childlessness needed to be something irreversible by modern medical miracles.

A Fruitless Crown

In Act IV, scene iii, on learning that Macbeth has slaughtered his entire family, Macduff cries out, 'He has no children.' In Act I, scene vii Lady Macbeth says, 'I have given suck.' Macbeth is tormented by the idea of Banquo being 'father to a line of kings' while he himself is lumbered with 'a barren sceptre' and a 'fruitless crown'. That about sums up the data that Shakespeare gives on a subject that would end up motoring my performance.

According to Holinshed's *Chronicle*, Lady Macbeth had a son by an earlier marriage. To assume that this was the child whom Lady Macbeth had suckled would iron out some contradictions and leave the blame for infertility at Macbeth's door. It would also fuel Lady Macbeth's taunts about her husband's manhood. To begin with it seemed an attractive theory.

I have to emphasize at this point that I am not claiming to know Shakespeare's intentions. He left much unexplained and we can only assume that he meant to leave it that way. However, for each performer or director the questions need to be addressed. A playable path must be found. I can only record some of our own thinking. Other actors will draw different conclusions. They always have, and long may they do so.

One director I spoke to reckoned that Lady Macbeth is barren and that 'I have given suck' is a neurotic fantasy that Macbeth allows her. In Kurosawa's film *Throne of Blood* (1957) Lady Macbeth is pregnant and loses the child at the banquet. Every production has to find a solution. Scholars' concerns lie elsewhere. One footnote I read dismissed the question of

Lady Macbeth's child or children as 'unprofitable'. That editor did not have to play the part.

Jan Kott is more understanding about the needs of performance. On whether or not the Macbeths have children he writes: 'This is not the most important factor in the interpretation of the tragedy, although it may be decisive for the interpretation of their parts by the two principal actors.' We found it to be so as soon as we started to put Act I, scene vii on its feet.

Tony had the problem of moving from 'We will proceed no further in this business' to 'I am settled, and bend up / Each corporal agent to this terrible feat' in as long as it took us to speak forty-seven lines. Consider the following:

Enter LADY MACBETH

MACBETH

      How now! what news?

LADY MACBETH

He has almost supp'd. Why have you left the chamber?

MACBETH

Hath he ask'd for me?

LADY MACBETH

      Know you not, he has?

MACBETH

We will proceed no further in this business:
He hath honour'd me of late; and I have bought
Golden opinions from all sorts of people,
Which would be worn now in their newest gloss,
Not cast aside so soon.

LADY MACBETH

      Was the hope drunk,
Wherein you dress'd yourself? Hath it slept since?
And wakes it now, to look so green and pale

At what it did so freely? From this time
Such I account thy love. Art thou afeard
To be the same in thine own act and valour,
As thou art in desire? Would'st thou have that
Which thou esteem'st the ornament of life,
And live a coward in thine own esteem,
Letting 'I dare not' wait upon 'I would,'
Like the poor cat i' th' adage?

MACBETH

      Pr'ythee, peace.
I dare do all that may become a man;
Who dares do more, is none.

LADY MACBETH

      What beast was't then,
That made you break this enterprise to me?
When you durst do it, then you were a man;
And, to be more than what you were, you would
Be so much more the man. Nor time, nor place,
Did then adhere, and yet you would make both:
They have made themselves, and that their fitness now
Does unmake you. I have given suck, and know
How tender 'tis to love the babe that milks me:
I would, while it was smiling in my face,
Have pluck'd my nipple from his boneless gums,
And dash'd the brains out, had I so sworn
As you have done to this.

MACBETH

      If we should fail?

LADY MACBETH

      We fail!
But screw your courage to the sticking-place,
And we'll not fail. When Duncan is asleep
(Whereto the rather shall his day's hard journey

Soundly invite him), his two chamberlains
Will I with wine and wassail so convince,
That memory, the warder of the brain,
Shall be a fume, and the receipt of reason
A limbeck only: when in swinish sleep
Their drenched natures lie, as in a death,
What cannot you and I perform upon
Th' unguarded Duncan? what not put upon
His spongy officers, who shall bear the guilt
Of our great quell?

MACBETH

       Bring forth men-children only!
For thy undaunted mettle should compose
Nothing but males. Will it not be receiv'd,
When we have mark'd with blood those sleepy two
Of his own chamber, and us'd their very daggers,
That they have done't?

LADY MACBETH

       Who dares receive it other,
As we shall make our griefs and clamour roar
Upon his death?

MACBETH

       I am settled, and bend up
Each corporal agent to this terrible feat.
Away, and mock the time with fairest show:
False face must hide what the false heart doth know.
Exeunt.

(Act I, scene vii)

Macbeth's turnaround was my problem too. Sarah Siddons
(1755–1831) decided that Lady Macbeth had to be so 'capti-
vating in feminine loveliness' and to have 'such potency as to
fascinate a hero . . . to seduce him to brave all the dangers of

the present and . . . the terrors of a future world'. So sheer sex-appeal then? Maybe Siddons could do that, but few if any others could seduce an entire audience along with Macbeth (for nothing less would be required in order to convince).

I then voiced my problem about the 'giving suck' line. Was it Macbeth's child? If so, is there hope of having more? If it was Macbeth's stepchild and Macbeth is infertile, then the answer is 'No'. What of Macbeth's 'Bring forth men-children only'? Is this a realistic suggestion? If they could have more children, why is Banquo's fecundity so threatening? These were stumbling blocks, but as is often the case, the actors' need to find a way to play the scene produced answers that were more revealing than if we had not stumbled at all.

In dramatic terms the stepson is a no-no. He plays an important part in the real history so why is he not in the play? Answer: Shakespeare is not interested in him. Forget him, then, and imagine the infant Lady Macbeth talks of to be Macbeth's. Where is that child? It could be a girl, I suppose, and therefore no good as heir to the throne, or it could have been a boy who died.

This seemed to us the most likely and contained the richest theatrical juice. But how, I protested, could a woman who knows 'How tender 'tis to love the babe that milks me', and has seen that baby die, even contemplate the thought of dashing an infant's brains out? I had fallen into the trap of seeing this violent image as proof of Lady Macbeth's heartlessness. But once I started to act the scene and feel the desperate energy of it, I understood that the opposite was the case. Lady Macbeth is thinking up the supreme, most horrendous sacrifice imaginable to her in order to shame her husband into keeping his pledge. She never has to match deeds to her words, but to dare to speak such pain-laden words is in itself impressive, and Macbeth realizes what it costs her.

To create the highest stakes possible for the couple in this short but pivotal scene, we decided that the couple had not spoken of the child since its death and that, for whatever reasons, they could not have any more. I argued for more than one dead child (a fairly normal tragedy in Shakespeare's day) – surely then she would feel truly blighted and perhaps vengeful against the world. In a morning's work we had solved Macbeth's volte-face for Tony, found a deep connection between the two characters, and I had found the heart of Lady Macbeth.

Nature and Heaven have outlawed her, so what does she owe to them? Her breasts are a cruel mockery, so why should the spirits not take her 'milk for gall'? (Interviewed in *Clamorous Voices*, Sinead Cusack decided that Lady Macbeth does a deal with the spirits, forfeiting her fertility in return for the crown*. I played the part a lot later in my life than Sinead did, so the sacrifice would have had less potency – an example of how seldom one actor can borrow another's good idea for the same part.)

I consulted a bereavement counsellor about the effects on the parents of losing a child. In some cases it bonds the couple more strongly than ever; in others the marriage cracks under a mixture of unspoken blame, guilt and grief not shared in a desire to protect the partner from a double burden.

Was I bending things too much to think that Shakespeare does not explain the couple's loss because they themselves cannot speak of it? A more likely scenario for a pre-Freudian playwright is that, although his writing supports psychoanalytical scrutiny, Shakespeare somehow created the depth and truth of his characters without recourse to any such science. In any case, it was not in his interests to stress any mitigating

* *Clamorous Voices*, The Women's Press (1988).

circumstances in Lady Macbeth's life. Nor was I trying to excuse Lady Macbeth by suggesting that it was normal for a bereaved parent to develop a vengeful spirit; but I was relieved to find a very human source for her actions, and I would grab at any chance of putting this across.

Jan Kott and others have suggested that Lady Macbeth's domineering and obsessional relationship with Macbeth represents a redirecting of her thwarted maternal feelings towards her husband. It is a view I acknowledge but which was never uppermost in my thoughts while I played. The discovery for me was that I could not satisfactorily relate to the idea of hunger for power in the abstract. Her ambition had to be driven by something more personal and deeper.

At the start of the play, might not Lady Macbeth be in a deep depression from which she is rescued by a new-found purpose that might restore meaning to her marriage? Winning the crown would not only give the couple the 'solely sovereign sway and masterdom' that so excites them, but it would give Lady Macbeth a role. She may not be able to nurture her husband's children but she can fix things for him to be king.

On Macbeth's return from the war, Greg discouraged tactile shows of affection between husband and wife (bereavement like theirs can lead to a physical coolness), and they greeted one another at arm's length. During the pause after 'never / Shall sun that morrow see', a servant brought on a bucket of water, a cloth and a towel, and I set about washing my husband's face and arms. In performance this served several functions: it increased the tension of having to shut up in front of the servant; it provided a moment of unerotic domestic intimacy; it wiped the blood and grime of battle off Tony's face, thus helping his quick change into the next scene; and it afforded Lady Macbeth a clearer reading of her husband's state of mind. It also set up the theme of hand-washing that is threaded through the play.

Greg helped me again in the staging of the next scene (Act I, scene vi), where Lady Macbeth welcomes the King's party. To make up maximum numbers, nearly the whole cast entered and filled the stage, among them Macduff, his young son and Lady Macduff with a baby in her arms. This image of happy families scorches Lady Macbeth for a second. I tried to make this moment register with a well-placed look, but I couldn't hope to communicate this complex story in a blink that the audience was not looking out for.

For rehearsal purposes we gave each scene a title (for example, 'Sleepwalking' is easier to identify than 'Act V, scene i'). Thus Act I, scene vii became 'Cold Feet'. I would listen from the wings as Macbeth, in soliloquy, reasoned his way out of our pact. It struck me that he was more concerned about his action rebounding against himself, and about other people's vilification, than about the morality of regicide or his pity for the King. He more or less states that if there were no consequences to his action he would not hesitate:

> that but this blow
> Might be the be-all and the end-all – here . . .
> We'd jump the life to come.

So much for the milk of human kindness; he is more worried about covering his back! – or so I thought as I waited to go on. In the wings was the life-like doll that had just been in Lady Macduff's arms. Its weight was disconcertingly real as I held it. I did not do this every night, but it was a useful touchstone for the raw fury that I would have to summon up in a few seconds' time.

> I have no spur
> To prick the sides of my intent, but only
> Vaulting ambition . . .

I hear Macbeth say this and, on cue in every sense of the word, rush on to spur him some more.

Lady Macbeth has little time for his fake surprise: 'Hath he [Duncan] ask'd for me?' 'Know you not, he has?' she smashes back.

When he breaks it to her that 'We shall proceed no further in this business', she explodes like a primed cannon. She disdains his lame excuse that, after he has just been honoured, the timing is inappropriate. She confronts him with exactly the faults she has listed behind his back in soliloquy: his wanting something for nothing, his lack of resolve, his cowardice. He hides behind some code of manhood (which the audience would not dispute), but she is not having it. She knows his real nature.

In most of us law-abiding citizens the Beast is kept under the control of the Man. To Lady Macbeth this is hypocrisy. 'Act out your fantasies. Own up to the whole of what you are. Anything less is weak,' she seems to say.

Within this interchange lie several important textual clues that are easily missed in the desperate heat of the argument. They provide my sliver of defence against all those who think of Macbeth as a nice guy enticed to murder by his wife. Examine the evidence (my emphases):

LADY MACBETH

> What beast was't then,
> That made *you* break this enterprise to *me*?
> When you durst *do it*, then you were a man . . .
> . . . Nor time, nor place,

Did *then* adhere, and yet *you would make both*:
They have made themselves, and that their fitness now
Does unmake you.

And at the end of the speech:

> . . . had I so sworn
> *As you have done to this.*

We have not heard him swear to anything, so it must have happened offstage. There must have been a discussion about doing 'it' at a point before 'time and place' were fitting, i.e. before Duncan came to stay – ergo, before the start of the play – and it was *he* who broke the enterprise to *her*. I rest my case.

Macbeth knows this to be true and is weakening, and at that moment his wife produces her trump card. That is one way of playing 'I have given suck . . ', or it could be a completely uncalculated outburst that takes even Lady Macbeth by surprise. I chose to play something between the two – something that started as a rational argument but that overwhelmed her in speaking it. Suddenly all her anger and sorrow well up.

As she sees it, she would have liked to be 'full o' th' milk of human kindness', but life has hardened her through no fault of her own. Macbeth's moral equivocation is a luxury that she resents. He can still hold his head up in his field. He receives honours. He may be a brave soldier when the rules are straightforward, but he is a moral coward in her eyes. He cannot match the courage she has built to face each childless day. As a childless wife she has no status. She feels superfluous and dried up. Nothing less than reigning as his queen can fill the hole in her life.

Her subconscious throws up the terrible image of killing her child and Macbeth is won over. Only something this enormous could have got him back on course. His simple 'If we should fail?' is as good as a promise to Lady Macbeth and, having chosen such an emotional interpretation for the previous speech, she has (as I did) some recovery problems for the reply, 'We fail.'

Unbeknownst to me at the time, this line is famously controversial. I would later be grilled about it in after-show discussions. In some editions it is punctuated as a question; in others not. How did I think of it? I answered that I varied the playing of it according to how quickly Lady Macbeth bounced back from what she had just gone through. The line contained relief that Macbeth was back on board, a challenge to him not to fail, and also perhaps a touch of nihilism – a 'what have we got to lose?' Macbeth might have answered, 'Quite a lot,' but life as it stands has little to offer her.

Then follows her garbled plan. She has barely thought it through. In Act I, scene v she has mentioned '*my* keen knife'; now she asks: 'What cannot *you and I* perform . . .?' and talks of '*our* great quell' (my emphases). So who exactly is going to do the killing, and how? We shall see how unprepared they are in a few scenes' time. Meanwhile Macbeth, genuinely moved by his wife's force of feeling, rewards her with: 'Bring forth men-children only'. Is he indulging her with hope against hope? or is he momentarily blinded by his own?

In the event, Duncan's murder is carried out by Macbeth in Act II, scene ii. Lady Macbeth's job is to get the King's bodyguards drunk and ring the bell to alert Macbeth when the time is right. Lady Macbeth gives a clue that she is not quite the tough nut she would like to be with her line: 'Had he not resembled / My father as he slept, I had done't'; or is this a rather flimsy dramatic device to keep her away from the scene until the crucial moment when she sees the 'gash'd stabs' on Duncan's corpse?

Macbeth emerges from the King's chamber and a hissed 'My husband!' alerts him to his wife waiting in the dark shadows. He rushes to join her. 'I have done the deed.'

They must whisper for fear of waking the house. They are bungling amateurs and trip over one another's words.

MACBETH
> Didst thou not hear a noise?

LADY MACBETH
I heard the owl scream, and the crickets cry.
Did not you speak?

MACBETH
> When?

LADY MACBETH
> Now.

MACBETH
> As I descended?

LADY MACBETH
Ay.

MACBETH
Hark!–

and so on. The panicky rhythms of this passage almost play themselves.

Then Macbeth starts to crack, his speeches spilling over with terror. His terror is terrifying for Lady Macbeth to behold, but she smothers her own panic in an attempt to control his: 'These deeds must not be thought / After these ways: so, it will make us mad.'

He raves wildly on, about a voice crying, 'Macbeth does murder Sleep . . . Macbeth shall sleep no more!'

She stops the torrent for a moment. 'Who was it that thus cried?' – in other words 'It's all in your head. Pull yourself together.'

'Go, get some water,' she commands, 'And wash this filthy witness from your hand.' Then her blood freezes:

> Why did you bring these daggers from the place?
> They must lie there: go, carry them, and smear
> The sleepy grooms with blood.

He refuses to look again on the crime. 'Pish!' she thinks, 'I'll go then. How can you be frightened of the dead and the sleeping?' She charges back up the stairs (in our production) and Macbeth is left alone with his remorse and his blood-soaked hands. What's done cannot be undone.

In that scene offstage in Duncan's chamber, a scene that, but for Macbeth's forgetfulness would not have happened, Lady Macbeth is confronted with the deed she has only talked of. From that moment her exterior aplomb will grow more and more brittle until it breaks.

I chose to make her faint in Act II, scene iii a genuine one, and it happens shortly after Macbeth describes the murder scene: 'Here lay Duncan, / His silver skin lac'd with his golden blood.' A flashback to the terrible sight, coupled with a sense of panic, is enough to overwhelm her. Her husband is wildly improvising and she has no control over his text.

There is a good case for her pretending to faint in order to distract from her husband's rather overstated performance, but I wanted to follow through with my theory that she, like Macbeth, was in shock.

The next time we see the couple they are crowned, and we will see their positions reverse. The dominant lady becomes the ruler's consort. Macbeth's focus has moved on to Banquo. Duncan's heirs have fled under suspicion of their father's murder and Banquo is now Macbeth's chief rival. In Act I, scene iv, Duncan honoured the two friends equally:

> Noble Banquo,
> That hast no less [than Macbeth] deserv'd, nor must be
>   known
> No less to have done so ...

Banquo alone knows the witches' full prophesy and he also knows Macbeth too well for Macbeth's comfort. Lady Macbeth gets little of her husband's attention. Her one line in Act III, scene i is a mere politeness and seems mainly to serve as an in-joke for Shakespeare: 'If he had been forgotten, / It had been as a gap in our great feast ...' There will indeed be a gap at the feast: Banquo's empty chair.

Macbeth and Banquo warily exchange chat and Macbeth learns that Banquo and his son will be out riding before dinner. There was a strong suggestion in our production that Banquo was heading off to see the witches. Who is not a little tempted to grasp at power once it comes within range or to let his integrity slip when others are playing a dirty game and seem to be winning? Lady Macbeth is aware of an atmosphere between the friends; she may even detect a hint of what underlies it. She dutifully takes a back seat, allowing her husband to establish his authority. Tony Sher was quite a bit shorter than Joseph O'Connor, who played Duncan, and as he now wore the same costume, it did indeed 'Hang loose about him, like a giant's robe / Upon a dwarfish thief,' the physical realization of Angus's later metaphor for his kingship (Act V, scene ii).

Macbeth suddenly dismisses the company: 'We will keep ourself till supper-time alone'. 'Ourself' not 'ourselves': Lady Macbeth can't help noticing the abrupt cut-off. She hovers, bewildered. 'While then, God be with you', he says, as if telling her 'and that includes you'. As she exits, she just catches Macbeth summoning his servant and realizes she is being excluded from something important. (It is possible to play

Lady Macbeth as a knowing accomplice throughout this scene, but this reading soon runs into trouble.)

Before his interview with the men hired to murder Banquo, Macbeth soliloquizes on the bitter joke whereby the crown, which has cost him his soul in the gaining, will be handed on to Banquo's progeny. Listening from offstage, I felt an unspoken accusation. If I had been a better mother . . .

The next scene (Act III, scene ii, which we dubbed 'Scorpions') was for both of us the most slippery scene in the play. Ostensibly it neither advances the plot nor tells the audience anything they don't already know. The couple use more than usually tender language to one another ('Gentle my Lord', 'Love . . . dear wife . . .'), but it is as a smokescreen or a means of control rather than as an expression of love. Committing a murder together has bound them in an almost erotic intimacy, but a new lack of trust has crept under their dialogue.

Picking up from Macbeth's entrance, Act III, scene ii reads as follows:

Enter MACBETH

LADY MACBETH

How now, my Lord? why do you keep alone,
Of sorriest fancies your companions making,
Using those thoughts, which should indeed have died
With them they think on? Things without all remedy
Should be without regard: what's done is done.

MACBETH

We have scorch'd the snake, not kill'd it:
She'll close, and be herself; whilst our poor malice
Remains in danger of her former tooth.
But let the frame of things disjoint, both the worlds suffer,
Ere we will eat our meal in fear, and sleep
In the affliction of these terrible dreams,

That shake us nightly. Better be with the dead,
Whom we, to gain our peace, have sent to peace,
Than on the torture of the mind to lie
In restless ecstasy. Duncan is in his grave;
After life's fitful fever he sleeps well;
Treason has done his worst: nor steel, nor poison,
Malice domestic, foreign levy, nothing
Can touch him further!

LADY MACBETH
          Come on:
Gentle my Lord, sleek o'er your rugged looks;
Be bright and jovial among your guests to-night.

MACBETH
So shall I, Love; and so, I pray, be you.
Let your remembrance apply to Banquo:
Present him eminence, both with eye and tongue:
Unsafe the while, that we
Must lave our honours in these flattering streams,
And make our faces vizards to our hearts,
Disguising what they are.

LADY MACBETH
          You must leave this.

MACBETH
O, full of scorpions is my mind, dear wife!
Thou know'st that Banquo, and his Fleance, lives.

LADY MACBETH
But in them Nature's copy's not eterne.

MACBETH
There's comfort yet; they are assailable:
Then be thou jocund. Ere the bat hath flown
His cloister'd flight; ere to black Hecate's summons
The shard-born beetle, with his drowsy hums,
Hath rung Night's yawning peal, there shall be done

A deed of dreadful note.

LADY MACBETH
What's to be done?

MACBETH
Be innocent of the knowledge, dearest chuck,
Till thou applaud the deed. Come, seeling Night,
Scarf up the tender eye of pitiful Day,
And, with thy bloody and invisible hand,
Cancel, and tear to pieces, that great bond
Which keeps me pale! – Light thickens; and the crow
Makes wing to th' rooky wood;
Good things of Day begin to droop and drowse,
Whiles Night's black agents to their preys do rouse.
Thou marvell'st at my words: but hold thee still;
Things bad begun make strong themselves by ill.
So, pr'ythee, go with me.
Exeunt.

In soliloquy before they meet, husband and wife echo one
another's sentiments:

MACBETH
To be thus is nothing, but to be safely thus.
(Act III, scene i)

LADY MACBETH
Nought's had, all's spent,
Where our desire is got without content:
'Tis safer to be that which we destroy,
Than by destruction dwell in doubtful joy.
(Act III, scene ii)

But when in her presence Macbeth says,

Better be with the dead,
Whom we, to gain our peace, have sent to peace,

Than on the torture of the mind to lie
In restless ecstasy,

Lady Macbeth gives no word or sign of agreement.

There is already a difference between their states of mind. His soliloquy develops into a plan to ease his anxiety, while hers expresses an emptiness with no remedy. It is a rare confession of despair, which she quickly converts into tough talk for Macbeth's benefit: 'Things without all remedy / Should be without regard: what's done is done.' Her seeming denial of the problem only alienates him further.

The problem is Banquo, and he cannot spell it out. But why can't Macbeth confide in his wife? Because he has decided on a course and doesn't want her to argue him out of it? Because he no longer trusts her after her faint and anyway, the fewer people involved the better? Because he is about to kill his best friend and cannot look at his own feelings in the mirror of her shocked face? Any of these could be true, but Tony needed to answer the question more specifically, and once again a seeming obstacle led us to a deeper layer of truth.

In his letter to his wife in Act I, scene v, Macbeth says nothing of the witches' prophesy for Banquo, and there is no other textual indication that Lady Macbeth learns of it later. One reason could be that Macbeth wants to put it from his mind and go for the bird in the hand; but another might be that he wants to shield his wife from the knowledge that their reign is to be a childless dead end. The fact that the witches have so far got things right makes their prediction for Banquo more and more credible and the prospect of more children for the Macbeths ever bleaker.

It takes some nerve to hold on to an assumption like this, especially when Shakespeare offers no explicit proof that this is what he had in mind; but it offered us a psychological coherence. The scene, which had felt like a hiatus at first, ended up propelling us further apart and further into the hell of the play.

As it begins, both characters want to reconnect, but her need is greater than his. She is defined by his need for her, and that has diminished. Because he cannot be totally honest with her, he is starting to go it alone. The balance of power between them has tipped irreversibly. In the reverse pattern to the one that characterized their earlier scenes together, Macbeth has long speeches while Lady Macbeth slips in the odd one-liner.

She listens to his outpourings but cannot quite follow their tortuous path. 'We have scorch'd the snake, not kill'd it,' he says. Who is the snake? Not Duncan, for they have killed him.

'She'll close, and be herself; whilst our poor malice / Remains in danger of her former tooth.' She gets the general gist – that a crime won't lie down – a sense of a harm not yet rooted out, even a sarcastic mockery of her own apparent calm: 'But let the frame of things disjoint, both the worlds suffer, / Ere we will eat our meal in fear . . .'

She tries to pull him together in her old practical style with: 'Be bright and jovial among your guests tonight,' and he seizes on the chance to bring up Banquo's name:

So shall I, Love; and so, I pray, be you.
Let your remembrance apply to Banquo:
Present him eminence, both with eye and tongue

(throwing back her own instruction to him in Act I, scene v: 'bear welcome in your eye, / Your hand, your tongue').

In performance Tony suddenly broke off at this point. Macbeth knows that Banquo won't be at the feast and he can't go on with the lie to his wife. Tony delivered the remaining,

> Unsafe the while, that we
> Must . . . make our faces vizards to our hearts,
> Disguising what they are,

with a sad perusal of my face as if to say, 'And here am I, disguising my true self even from *you*!'

She clings to her old role of comforter, of rallier, but her grasp is less secure. Her part as co-conspirator seems to have been written out.

Macbeth gives a tiny hint of his plans: 'Thou know'st that Banquo, and his Fleance, lives.'

A slight pause while she thinks: 'Have I got this right . . .?' and then, more concerned to show her husband that she is as sharp as ever than to know why he would kill his friend, she tentatively offers: 'But in them Nature's copy's not eterne' (innocent of the irony of the line), which provides Macbeth with the go-ahead he still needs her to give. However, when she probes further with: 'What's to be done?', the former 'partner of greatness' is fobbed off with a patronizing: 'Be innocent of the knowledge, dearest chuck, / Till thou applaud the deed.' The Lady Macbeth of earlier scenes would have protested, would have wrung an explanation out of him; but she says nothing for the rest of the scene.

For me this silence confirmed my theory that Lady Macbeth's ambition is not ambition for power's sake but for her husband and for their marriage. As far as she is concerned, they have achieved what they wanted, but 'Nought's had', if they cannot enjoy it together. She can put the murder behind her (or she thinks she can), but Macbeth's fretting is destroying everything. If they drift apart, her purpose is lost, and therein lay all her strength.

Macbeth seems to soliloquize in front of her, almost unaware of her presence. With a mixture of anger, excitement and dread, she listens and watches from the perimeter while Macbeth stokes himself up for some dreadful deed at which she only dimly guesses. Banquo is to die – that much she gathers – but the husband she thought she knew would not kill his closest friend; at least not without her courage to sustain him. Evidently he has moved on.

Not being privy to his motives, she is all the more dismayed by the thought of what's to be done. When Macbeth snaps out of his musing, he interprets her demeanour as astonishment – 'Thou marvell'st at my words' – and, as if to prevent her interrupting, continues, 'but hold thee still; / Things bad begun make strong themselves by ill.'

In Tony's performance, that 'bad begun' was loaded with the implication: 'You got me into this. You made me into this murderer'; and I/Lady Macbeth felt the sting of his hatred as he swept past me and almost left the stage. At the last minute he turned back to interrupt my perturbed reverie with a brusquely extended hand and 'So, pr'ythee go with me.'

Stepp'd in so Far

The jaggedness of this last exit informs the atmosphere at the top of Act III, scene iv (or 'Dinner with the Ceauçescus', as we flippantly called it). The lights find the pair sitting stiffly side by side, forearms resting on the table top in four parallel lines. They stare ahead with haunted eyes. In keeping with the rest of the set design this feast was to be Brechtian/austere: eight tin bowls awaiting a dribble of soup, some cutlery, a rough loaf with a knife to cut it, and six guttering candles furnishing the only light. Into this gloom crept the somewhat cowed guests, each clutching a wine-filled goblet. Macbeth's is already a nervous court.

Tony's Macbeth jumped to his feet to welcome them and, in what is often played as an aside to his wife, took the chance publicly to offset himself against his wife as the approachable People's King:

> Ourself will mingle with society,
> And play the humble host.
> Our hostess keeps her state; but, in best time,
> We will require her welcome.

'Sorry about my snotty wife,' he seems to say, mocking her tense attitude, though his was identical seconds before. It is an effective betrayal and a taunt: 'You wanted me to be jolly. You taught me to dissemble. Who's the better at it now?'

But his cockiness is short-lived. Banquo's murderer appears and the host is forced to leave the table without a toast. When he returns, his queen can get her own back, publicly but graciously correcting him, and throwing in the odd guest-pleasing witticism for good measure:

>   My royal Lord,
> You do not give the cheer: the feast is sold,
> That is not often vouch'd, while 'tis a-making,
> 'Tis given with welcome: to feed were best at home;
> From thence, the sauce to meat is ceremony;
> Meeting were bare without it.

Macbeth has just learnt that Banquo is dead but that his son Fleance has escaped. He nevertheless manages a charming show:

>   Sweet remembrancer! –
> Now, good digestion wait on appetite,
> And health on both!

But the nightmare will out. With the appearance of Banquo's ghost Macbeth goes to pieces and his wife briefly returns to her old commanding form. Her rationality ('This is the very painting of your fear . . . When all's done, / You look but on a stool') and her taunts ('O! these flaws and starts / (Impostors to true fear), would well become / A woman's story . . .') quieten Macbeth a little, but with each fresh apparition of the ghost he grows less controllable and lets more and more cat out of the bag.

Despite Lady Macbeth's brilliantly improvised cover-ups, the guests are not fooled. Depending on each lord's degree of suspicion, Macbeth is either mad or in deep trouble. How are they to interpret Macbeth's speech into the empty air?

>   If thou canst nod, speak too. –
> If charnel-houses and our graves must send
> Those that we bury, back, our monuments
> Shall be the maws of kites.

No one yet knows of Banquo's murder, but Macbeth is already suspected by some of having killed Duncan. (There are hints of this in Macduff's attitude in Act II, scene iv, and more in Act III, scene vi.)

Thanks to Lady Macbeth's efforts, Macbeth briefly comes to his senses and apologizes to the assembly:

Do not muse at me, my most worthy friends,
I have a strange infirmity, which is nothing
To those that know me. Come, love and health to all.

One night in performance, Tony delivered that 'which is nothing / To those that know me' locking each guest in his threatening glare, as if to say: 'Anyone who speaks of this is a dead man.' Thereafter it was the only way to play the line. All pretence was over. An open reign of terror had begun.

Does the actor playing Banquo appear or not? Every production has to answer this question. Ours could have been accused of falling between two stools, because sometimes he did and sometimes he didn't. The inconsistency was deliberate; it caught the audience on the hop. At first they were like the guests witnessing their host raving at an empty stool, but just when they had settled to the idea of a 'ghost-less' production, they saw the ghost materialize from nowhere (a well-rehearsed trick) and were sucked inside Macbeth's head. (Sarah Siddons reasoned that Lady Macbeth knew she had endorsed Banquo's murder with 'But in them Nature's copy's not eterne', and therefore saw his ghost as well. This interpretation was recorded in one essay I read as: 'The last appearance of Banquo's ghost is also visible to Lady Macbeth, because it is she who has suggested to Macbeth the murder of Banquo and Fleance.' This from an academic! Had he somehow missed Macbeth's scene with the murderers?)

Lady Macbeth only knows for certain that Banquo is dead from her husband's over-frequent references to his absence from the feast. She is discomfited by Macbeth's uncalled-for 'Here had we now our country's honour roof'd, / Were the grac'd person of our Banquo present' early in the scene; but his later 'I drink . . . to our dear friend Banquo, whom we miss; / Would he were here! To all, and him, we thirst,' is one bluff too many.

When the ghost finally departs and Macbeth is 'a man again', Lady Macbeth gives him a cold and sarcastic 'You have displac'd the mirth, broke the good meeting / With most admir'd disorder.'

I felt that Lady Macbeth could not bring herself to look at her husband, for shame at his behaviour. This provoked Tony brutally to swing me round to face him, and punish my hypocrisy:

> You make me strange
> Even to the disposition that I owe,
> When now I think you can behold such sights,
> And keep the natural ruby of your cheeks,
> When mine is blanch'd with fear.

There is no saving the situation now. Lady Macbeth suddenly flips. Like a vicious bitch chasing intruders, she barks at the guests to get out, and the couple are left alone together, embarrassed, frightened and furious.

The tone of this last phase of the scene is curiously calm. There is a kind of detached intimacy between husband and wife. There are no recriminations or post-mortems. They have both blown it and there is nothing to discuss. Macbeth can ask the simple question: 'What is the night?' and she can answer: 'Almost at odds with morning, which is which.' They are at a mid-point (indeed the scene comes almost exactly halfway through the play) where night elides with day and their world slips into Hell. As Macbeth reasons,

> I am in blood
> Stepp'd in so far, that, should I wade no more,
> Returning were as tedious as go o'er.

He is preoccupied with the immediate future: done Banquo – who's next? Macduff? Why didn't he show up? He half-consults his wife on the matter, but they both know it makes no difference what she answers. Instead she offers her own desultory question: 'Did you send to him, Sir?'

As Macbeth mutters his plans to himself, his wife peruses this stranger for whom she has traded her soul, this serial murderer who could have taken shape only under her guiding hand. His torment leaves her cold. She is drained. Exhausted herself, she suggests: 'You lack the season of all natures, sleep.'

Then, one rehearsal, Tony looked at me and I looked at him and the lameness and absurdity of that line and the agony and horror of what we had done and what we had become burst spontaneously out of both of us with a terrible giggling laughter. We managed to re-create that moment every night. It was a last flash of togetherness before Macbeth leaves the room to wade deeper into crime and to become better at it.

> Come, we'll to sleep. My strange and self-abuse
> Is the initiate fear, that wants hard use:
> We are yet but young in deed.

He doesn't notice that his wife's laughter has shifted into a half-crazed whimpering.

I did not follow him to bed but took one of the candles from the table to light my separate path. We would not meet onstage again.

Sleep No More

'Sleep shall neither night nor day / Hang upon his penthouse lid' – thus the First Witch in Act I, scene iii, cursing the sailor to punish his wife.

Throughout *Macbeth* sleep is a yearned-for refuge reserved for the innocent and the dead. On the night of Duncan's murder, Banquo's 'A heavy summons lies like lead upon me, / And yet I would not sleep' signals a loss of trust. He cannot afford to relax his guard. Duncan innocently gives way to sleep and is murdered in his bed.

To kill a king is one thing; to kill a sleeping king is double vandalism, and Macbeth is to be punished in kind. It is the presentiment of this particular form of torture that obsesses Macbeth as he rushes from the scene of the crime:

Methought, I heard a voice cry, 'Sleep no more!
Macbeth does murder Sleep,' – the innocent Sleep;
Sleep, that knits up the ravell'd sleave of care,
The death of each day's life, sore labour's bath . . .

(Act II, scene ii)

Lady Macbeth cannot understand him, or she will not. She is more concerned with the real fear of discovery. Her narrow focus is her strength.

Later, when her purpose is lost with her love, she will suffer the irony of wakeful sleep. The 'access and passage to remorse' is unstopped and, like a creature in Hell, she must live out the actions of her crime till the ultimate sleep relieves her.

Macbeth, whose humanity has hitherto been measured by his self-honesty in soliloquy, progressively eschews deliberation: 'To crown my thoughts with acts, be it thought and done,' he declares at the end of Act IV, scene i, and with those words he condemns Macduff's family to death. It is as though he has absorbed his wife's lesson and taken it further than she could possibly have intended. Indeed, it is the murder of Macduff's wife and children that finally tips Lady Macbeth over the edge.

To soliloquize is to make the audience your friend and through them to have a dialogue with yourself. It keeps a character sane. Lady Macbeth is afforded no such luxury. In the whole play she has four lines of honest reflection on her state ('Nought's had, all's spent . . .' in Act III, scene ii). There are other moments that arguably might be shared with the audience and Greg offered me these, but to me they felt wrong. Her friendlessness seemed essential. Her sleepwalking is her release – her soliloquy, if you like – though sleep itself removes her from self-understanding.

'That William Shakespeare must have done a murder,' was the response of a convicted murderer who, in return for helping Tony in his research, had been invited to see *Macbeth* for the first time. By that token he must also have known about post-traumatic stress disorder. In a modern pamphlet on the subject I read of a young rape victim who 'could not sleep without a light by his bed'. The Doctor who witnesses Lady Macbeth's sleepwalking asks: 'How came she by that light?' to which the attending Gentlewoman answers: 'Why, it stood by her: she has light by her continually; 'tis her command.'

To attribute all of Shakespeare's psychological accuracy to first-hand experience is to diminish his dramatic artistry. God knows how he did it, but the sleepwalking scene (Act V, scene i) – its placement within the play, its pity and terror, its atmosphere, its naturalistic rhythms – is one of the most memorable scenes in the canon.

It comes after a long spell away from Macbeth's castle. The audience has been transported to the witches' cavern, heard the treble voices of children at Macduff's castle, reeled at their brutal murder, and spent time in England breathing a different air made lighter by the promise of revenge. Now the play is plunged into gloom again.

In a corridor of Macbeth's castle a Doctor and Gentlewoman lurk in the dark, their faces lit by one candle. The Gentlewoman has watched Lady Macbeth for several nights and has heard what she knows she should not. She needs to share her burden with a witness. The scene is charged with danger. Think Stalin's Russia, or some such, where it can be a death sentence to think a thought, let alone to speak it aloud.

The Doctor and Gentlewoman are interrupted in their hushed discussion by the entrance of Lady Macbeth. The actress is given clear stage directions by the whispered dialogue:

> How came she by that light? . . .
> You see, her eyes are open . . .
> What is it she does now? Look, how she rubs her hands . . .
> It is an accustom'd action with her, to seem thus washing her hands. I have known her continue in this a quarter of an hour.

Then the Lady speaks, and this presents something of an acting dilemma. I wanted the audience to feel they were eavesdropping on Lady Macbeth cocooned in her private Hell. Unconscious of listeners, she has no need to project and if I once started to 'perform' the scene, I would lose that reality. On the other hand, I had to be heard.

For most of the play Lady Macbeth's has been an acting job. She (and the actor playing her) must make a few central decisions, block out all other considerations, wind herself up and go. Night after night, like Lady Macbeth herself, I would forget the enormity of her crime and focus on the minute-to-minute crisis of each scene, until the sleepwalking scene knocked down our guard, letting the horrors break in.

I responded to the jump-cut rhythms of her speech, which have the effect of an incoherent dream. 'Out, damned spot! out, I say!' (The murder is done and she looks at her hands.) 'One; two: why, then 'tis time to do't.' (The murder is yet to be done. She is Macbeth, hearing the bell strike.) 'Hell is murky.' (Her present terror? or his?) 'Fie, my Lord, fie! a soldier, and afeard? What need we fear who knows it, when none can call our power to accompt?' (Talking down his fear or her own?)

Then the sudden flashback: 'Yet who would have thought the old man had so much blood in him?' which gives the Doctor his first inkling of what is being talked about. Jump-cut to the next horror: 'The Thane of Fife had a wife: where is she now?' (If one thane's wife can be killed, why not another?) Then immediately: 'What, will these hands ne'er be clean?' The Macduffs' blood is on her hands too. All Macbeth's crimes are her crimes, even this, for she helped create him.

Then another volte-face: 'No more o' that, my Lord, no more o' that: you mar all with this starting.' (It is her own starting that she condemns by transference – another insight into the bravado of her earlier scenes.)

The Doctor and Gentlewoman are terrified at what they are learning: 'you have known what you should not,' says the Doctor of his patient. 'Heaven knows what she has known,' returns the Gentlewoman. They do not yet contemplate what she might have done.

Through the thickness of her sleep Lady Macbeth still smells the blood on her hands and her deepest sighs come with the realization that 'all the perfumes of Arabia will not sweeten this little hand. Oh! oh! oh!'

Compare this with Macbeth's speech after Duncan's murder:

> Will all great Neptune's ocean wash this blood
> Clean from my hand? No, this my hand will rather
> The multitudinous seas incarnadine,
> Making the green one red.
>
> (Act II, scene ii)

The difference is that Macbeth confronts his nightmares waking.

The Doctor and the Gentlewoman express their compassion – 'I would not have such a heart in my bosom, for the dignity of the whole body' – despite what they guess at. The defencelessness of a sleepwalker is pitiable, even when she is Lady Macbeth, and therein lies the genius of the scene.

Lady Macbeth's 'Oh! oh! oh!' is the low point in her nightly-repeated cycle. She forces herself out of it with her wonted practicality, commanding her husband (or herself): 'Wash your hands, put on your night-gown; look not so pale. – I tell you yet again, Banquo's buried: he cannot come out on's grave.' A further revelation for the onlookers. Banquo too? 'Even so?'

Then the nightmare jumps back again in time, to Duncan's murder: 'there's knocking at the gate. Come, come, come, come, give me your hand.' Here I groped for the alarmed Doctor's hand. Is she awake or asleep? Then: ' What's done cannot be undone' – a modulation on her 'what's done is done' from the 'Scorpions' scene – and with an infinitely weary 'To bed, to bed, to bed,' she leaves as swiftly as she came.

The Doctor has detected something suicidal in her tone, for he requires the Gentlewoman to

> Look after her;
> Remove from her the means of all annoyance,
> And still keep eyes upon her.

But for all anyone's efforts, that bed does indeed become a welcome grave.

Strutting and Fretting

Meanwhile Macbeth, like Hitler in his last days in the bunker, must play out his destined 'hour upon the stage'. Despite his bluster he knows his cause is lost. What remains remarkable is his insight into his own brutalized condition.

> I have almost forgot the taste of fears . . .
> . . . I have supp'd full with horrors:
> Direness, familiar to my slaughterous thoughts,
> Cannot once start me.
>   (Act V, scene v)

The announcement of his wife's death only glancingly hurts him and the realization that he can feel so little for what he prized so much provokes the nihilism of the greatest speech in the play – 'Tomorrow, and tomorrow, and tomorrow . . .' Macbeth the philosopher is back for a moment, only to be lost in the mayhem of the final battle.

Most of his followers have defected to Malcolm's side, but Macbeth clings to the witches' promise that: 'none of woman born / Shall harm Macbeth' and

> Macbeth shall never vanquish'd be, until
> Great Birnam wood to high Dunsinane hill
> Shall come against him.
>   (Act IV, scene i)

The arrival of Malcolm's army camouflaged by the branches of Birnam wood knocks one prophecy out. One to go. Macbeth grows more reckless with each fading hope and when the last hope vanishes with Macduff's revelation that he was 'Untimely ripp'd' from his mother's womb, Macbeth roars into action. Macduff is fuelled by his unquenchable grief, while Macbeth has nothing but a death wish.

In our production, in the last throes of the fight, Macduff was momentarily disarmed but managed to grab a dagger. The sight of this new weapon recalled an earlier vision to Macbeth and, replicating the gesture he had used with the phantom dagger of Act II, scene i, he lashed out at the empty air around the weapon, as if it too were a hallucination. A violin bow scraping across a cymbal's rim re-created the unearthly sound that had heralded the earlier apparition. Taken off guard by his fevered brain, Macbeth was an easy final target for Macduff, in whose embrace he died.

Post-Mortem

Until I came to play her I did not understand why Lady Macbeth is supposed to be such a great role. She is out of the action for huge chunks of the play, has far fewer speeches than Macbeth and therefore fewer opportunities to explain herself. Macbeth on his own is unquestionably a great challenge for an actor, while Lady Macbeth on her own is less complex. But once you see her as dark twin, mirror, partner in crime to Macbeth (and if, as I did, you have a thrilling and intelligent actor to play opposite), she becomes the great role of repute.

A year after playing the part I am left with the feeling of having made a fist-sized dent in a battleship. I concentrated on finding the extremes to which a 'normal' person can be driven, rather than personifying an 'abnormal' psychopath. In the context of our production that was the coherent path. There are many others.

The normal person approach takes you on a bumpy ride. I had to dig around for anything I might have in common with Lady Macbeth – not a happy pastime. There is a fury inside me somewhere; there is a hunger and maybe even the capacity to kill. Am I unusual? Patently not. The point is that the condition of my life does not feed and sustain these qualities. Rage erupts and dies down. Hunger is kept at bay by a mostly satisfying life, and if I ever want to kill, the feeling lasts for a second and is quickly quelled by thinking of the consequences.

So is it only our circumstances that separate me from Lady Macbeth, or does the difference lie in the murkier area of our basic nature? And if as an actress I am able to re-mould my personality and even, to some degree, the inner workings of my imagination, how resilient is that basic nature of mine? In order to understand Lady Macbeth's motives I had begun to empathize with her, and empathy blurs moral judgement.

The major difference is that I only thought about the things she set in motion. In that sense perhaps we are all Macbeths, our crimes dormant until circumstances or a Lady Macbeth whip us up out of our law-abiding complacency.

Dunsinane (a Postscript)

At the beginning of September 2000 we wrapped up on a film of *Macbeth* for Channel 4. It was a year to the day since rehearsals had begun. The following weekend I happened to be invited to a christening in Scotland. At breakfast in my B&B I was leafing through a local guidebook and spotted 'Dunsinane' in the index.

'Oh, is that near here?' I asked my hostess.

She crossed the room and pointed out of the window at an unimposing hump in the distance. 'That's Dunsinane Hill,' she said (she pronounced it Dun*si*nan). There was a slightly more imposing hill right next to it, which was known as 'The King's Seat'.

After breakfast we drove the short distance to Dunsinane Hill and followed the road round the edge of the fields that led to the hill, looking for the gateway to a walk to the top that our hostess had described. Then the road started to sweep us away from the hill, so we turned round and tried again. We got out and walked, but we could not find the way in.

We went to the christening and, not to be beaten, tried again later in the day to make the approach to the hill. It would not let us in. We drove instead to Birnam Forest some fifteen minutes away and had an uneventful walk in what seemed a very ordinary wood. I gathered up a few twigs and presented them to Tony and Greg in London just for a joke. They hung them in the hall and, as far as I know, they are still there.

What had I expected from these places? For some spooky magic to rub off on me? To be somehow 'recognized' as kin by the earth and the trees? To find some insight into the 'real' Macbeths? The fact is that Shakespeare's is the 'real' Macbeth to us, and his story can be relived any day and in any place where people choose to act it out and watch it, from Toronto to Thailand to Timbuktu.

The 'true' story of Macbeth has been handed down according to the political bias of the chronicler. It has been as reworked and reinterpreted as any fiction, and the supposed geographical and historical landmarks of his life are mere dots on a map, signifying nothing.